THE BEST ADULT COLORING BOOK

FOR STRESS RELIEF AND RELAXATION

This Book Belongs To:

____

LOVE
LOVE
LOVE
LOVE

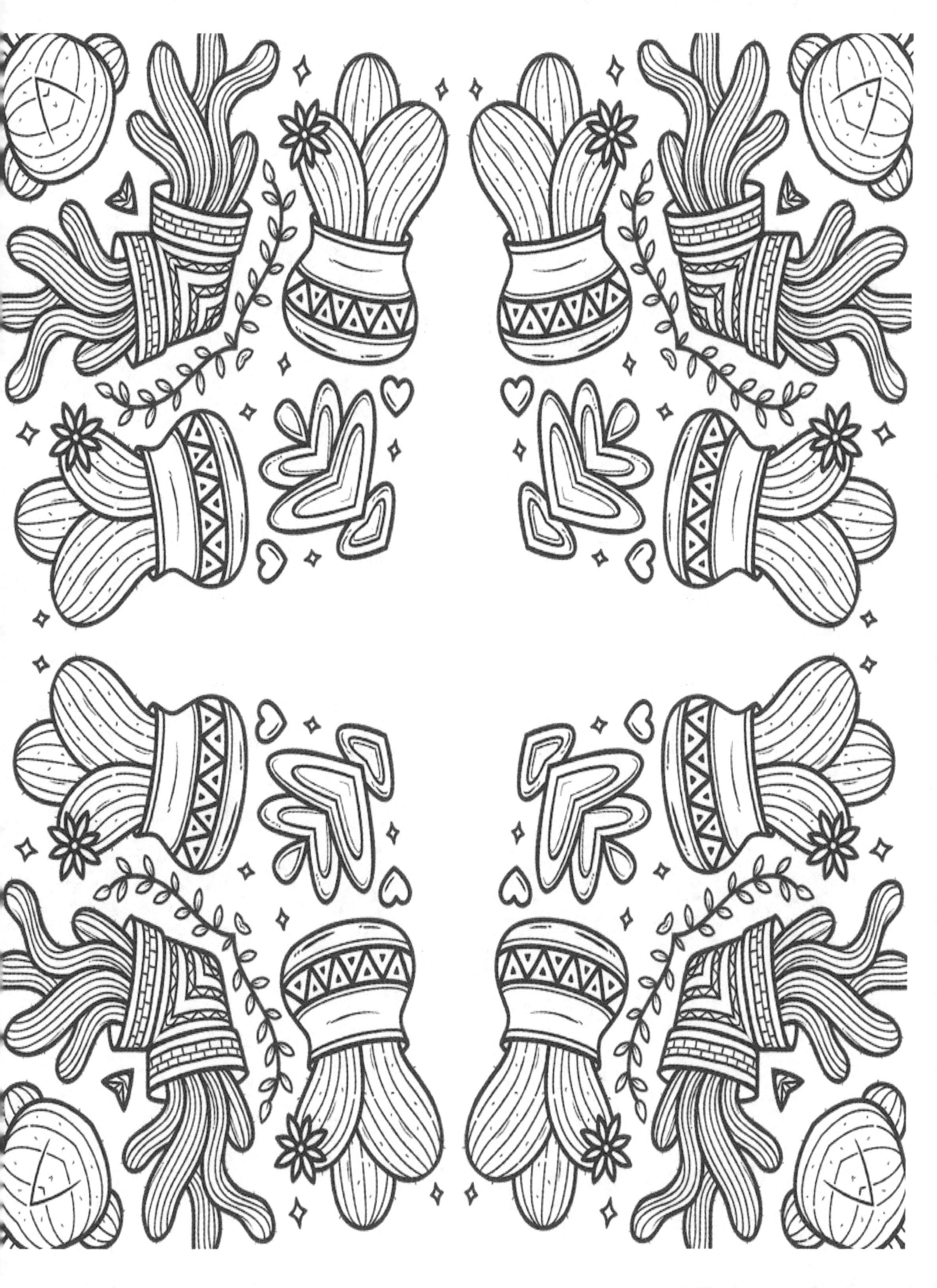

www.ingramcontent.com/pod-product-compliance
Lightning Source LLC
Chambersburg PA
CBHW081724250726
48657CB00010B/3122